A LITTLE HELP

Written by Alan A. Rubin
Illustrated by Tim Banks

Harcourt Achieve

Rigby • Saxon • Steck-Vaughn

www.HarcourtAchieve.com
1.800.531.5015

CONTENTS

TiME FOR A CHANGE

One night, Beaver looked around the pond where he had lived all his life. "Why does it suddenly seem so small?" he wondered.

His little brother and sister happily played tag in the bright moonlight. But Beaver didn't want to play. Instead, he climbed to the top of the dam and looked at the stream that stretched out before him. "Where does the stream lead?" Beaver asked his mom.

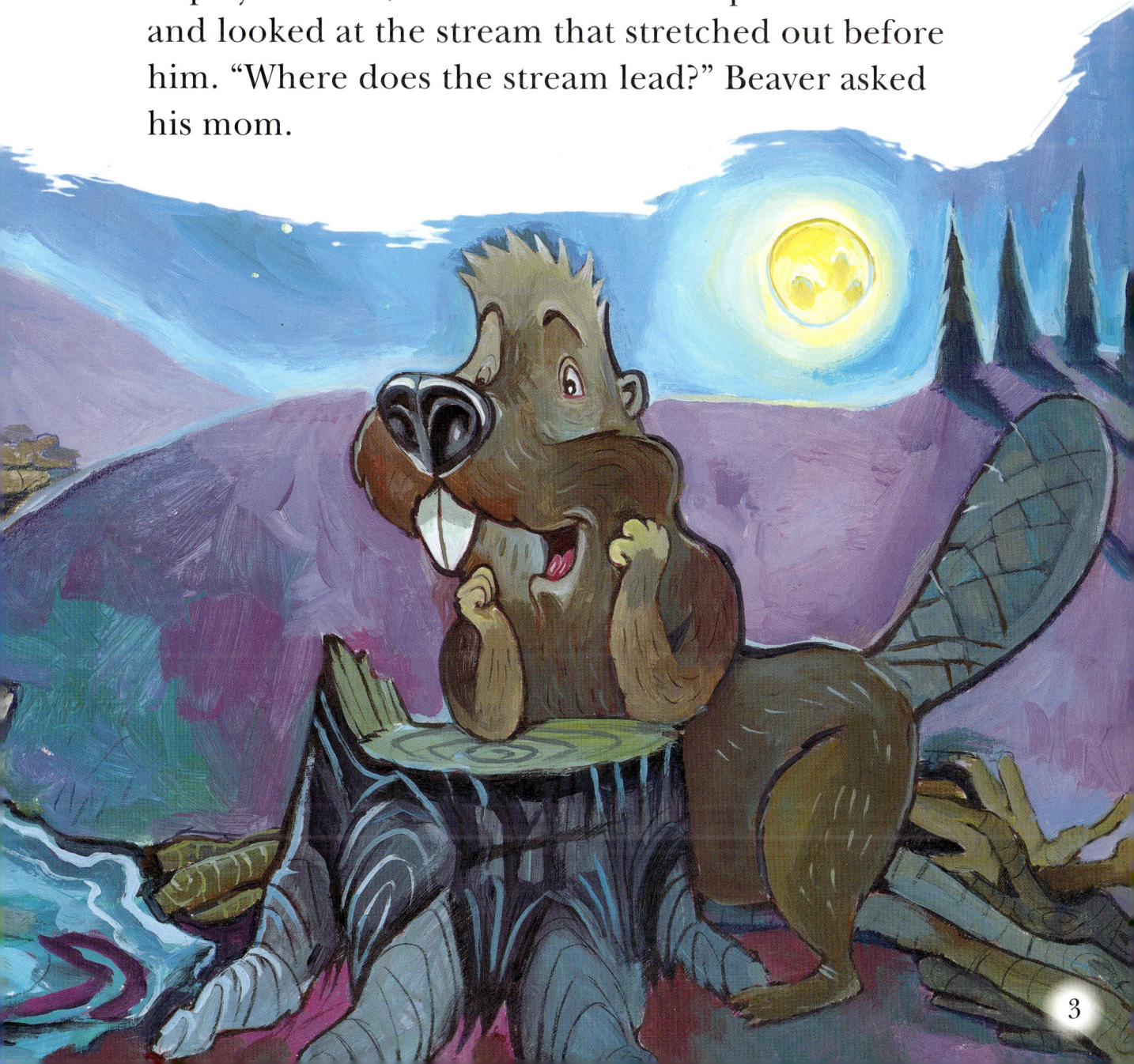

Beaver's mom and dad stopped working and joined Beaver at the top of the dam. Beaver's mom hugged him.

"Beaver, your father and I knew this day would come. You're all grown up now. There's only one way to find out where the stream leads," she said.

"Follow it!" Beaver's dad said. "That's what I did when I was your age."

So, that very night, Beaver said goodbye to his family and started off down the narrow stream.

For a while, Beaver waddled along beside the stream. When he got tired of walking, he tried to swim. But the stream was not deep enough.

Beaver was tired and hungry, so he stopped for a snack. He nibbled on the bark of a leafy branch. Then he dug a burrow in the soft ground and settled down to rest.

"Ahh!" Beaver thought, just before he fell asleep. "This spot is almost perfect! All it needs is some deep water for swimming. If only I could swim, I think I'd want to stay here forever!"

THE NEW POND

Beaver didn't get to rest very long. Some of the animals that lived nearby had come to meet him.

"Hey, Mister, are you a beaver?" Frog croaked.

"Of course he's a beaver," snapped Turtle. "What else could he be? Look at those teeth and that tail!"

"Yippee!" Frog cheered. "We're getting a pond! We're getting a pond!"

"We are?" Beaver yawned. "Great! I usually wake up around sunset. Let me know when the pond is ready. I'd love to take a swim." Beaver closed his eyes again and began snoring.

Beaver slept peacefully, dreaming about the new pond. When he woke up, Frog, Turtle, and other animals were standing around his burrow.

"Oh, hello!" Beaver said. "Is the pond ready?" Everyone laughed, everyone except Frog.

"We're not beavers. We don't know how to build ponds. That's *your* job!" Frog told Beaver. "Don't you think you should get started? We've been waiting all day!"

Beaver thought long and hard. "But how do I build a pond?" he asked.

"You mean you don't know how?" asked Frog, disappointed.

"Just do what beavers do best," said Turtle.

Beaver was best at building dams, so he began doing just that. Night after night, he gathered branches and piled them up to make a dam. He filled in the spaces between the branches with leaves, grass, and mud.

As the dam grew bigger, the flow of the stream became blocked. The water rose higher and higher behind the dam. Beaver had done it! He had made a pond! He was so proud.

Beaver's pond was beautiful and busy. Every day, animals came to paddle in the water and nibble on the plants that grew around the edges. While the others enjoyed the water, Beaver slept the day away in the cozy lodge he had built for himself, right in the middle of the pond.

At night, the pond was quieter. Beaver glided through the water and stared up at the stars. Each night, he also had a job to do. He had to fix any leaks in the dam. If he didn't, the water would leak out of the pond.

It would have been nice to have a little help, but no one offered. So Beaver worked alone.

A TERRIBLE TALE

One night, Beaver was feeling a little lonely. He remembered how his mom used to bring him the sweetest branches from the treetops.

He decided to cut down a tall tree, all by himself. He gnawed away near the bottom. The tree began to sway. "I can't wait to taste those leaves," Beaver thought.

But Beaver had made a terrible mistake. The wind was blowing hard, and Beaver was standing in the wrong place. . . .

Crash! The heavy tree fell right on Beaver's tail. The animals came running. Frog got Owl to examine Beaver's smashed tail.

Owl wrapped Beaver's tail in bandages. "Get right to bed!" Owl said firmly. "No work for at least a week!"

"But what about the dam?" Beaver asked. "It has to be checked every night! Who will make all the repairs?"

"Don't worry," Turtle said. "We'll work together to take care of the dam until you're better."

"Yup! You tell us what to do, and we'll do it," agreed Frog.

So, every night, Beaver's friends tried to fix the dam, but they weren't much help. Moose's antlers got in the way when he tried to check for cracks and leaks. Duck and Heron tripped when they tried to carry branches. Turtle got stuck in the mud on his way to the dam.

When Frog saw what trouble the others were in, she thought of a plan and quickly hopped away.

TO THE RESCUE

The animals had tried to help, but they had only made things worse. The dam was leaking!

A few nights later, Beaver tried to swim over and take a look, but he could barely move his tail.

"Ouch!" Beaver cried. "Even if I were well now, it would take an army of beavers to fix this dam before all of the water leaks away!"

Everyone was so worried about the dam that they didn't notice that Frog was back—until she spoke up.

"An army? How about a family? Surprise!" Frog said. Frog had hopped all the way to Beaver's old pond. She had brought Beaver's family back to help. They all got right to work. They chewed, carried, piled, and pushed. When they were done, the dam was stronger, and the pond was bigger and deeper than ever before.

Beaver's family stayed until his tail was healed. Beaver's mom and dad told him how proud they were that he had made such a nice home for himself. And they let him know that they would always be there for him.

After they left, Beaver's nights seemed more and more lonely. He found it hard to sleep. One morning, he stayed up to watch the sunrise. Suddenly, Beaver heard a lovely voice. It belonged to a beaver just his age!

"Excuse me," she said. "Do you mind if I build a lodge on your pond? It's so beautiful here!"

"Beautiful," Beaver gulped. "Of course, I don't mind! In fact, I hope you'll let me help you."

"Thanks," she answered. "I'd be glad to have a little help!"

Close AND Turn

Hoover Dam

Written by Alan A. Rubin

Harcourt Achieve
Rigby • Saxon • Steck-Vaughn

www.HarcourtAchieve.com
1.800.531.5015

Contents

Every year, millions of people visit Lake Mead in Nevada to swim, fish, camp, and go boating. They also visit the amazing **concrete** wall that stands at one end of the lake. It's Hoover **Dam**.

Hoover Dam is one of the largest dams in the world. Without it, Lake Mead wouldn't exist. But Hoover Dam has done a lot more than make a lake. It's changed the way farmers grow crops and the way cities get electricity and drinking water.

Let's take a look at how this huge dam was built and why.

View of Hoover Dam from above

Water, Water, Water

People can't live without water. So for a long time, very few people lived in desert areas of the southwestern United States. But the U.S. **government** wanted to change that. If deserts could get enough water, farmers could move there and grow crops. Roads and towns would be built around the farms.

To make this possible, workers dug **ditches** in the desert near the Colorado River. They connected the ditches to the powerful river. Water rushed through the ditches and poured onto the dry lands. Soon, there was enough water to grow fruit and vegetables!

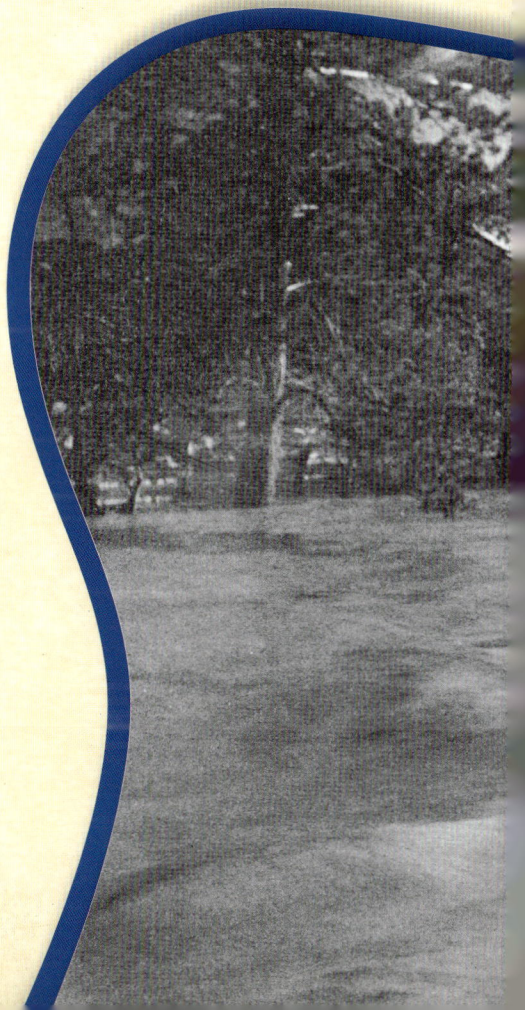

Then, in 1904, something terrible happened. **Floods**! Heavy rains caused the Colorado River to overflow. Too much water poured through the ditches. Farmers' crops, homes—even whole towns—were washed away. The rushing Colorado River was too strong. But people didn't want to move away. They fixed up their land and homes the best that they could and stayed near the river. Some years, the river was calm. Other years, there were more terrible floods.

There had to be a better way! Some people began talking about a dam. But could anyone build a dam big enough and strong enough to control the powerful Colorado River?

Floods, 1904

In 1918, people began planning to build this new dam. They wanted to build the dam across a tall, narrow **canyon**. It needed to be tall to hold back a lot of water. It needed to be narrow because it would take less time to build across a narrow canyon than a wider one.

Workers went out on the Colorado River, searching for the perfect spot. The area they chose had to be strong enough to keep the dam in place. Workers climbed dangerous canyons and tested rocks for years. They finally decided to build the dam across Black Canyon in Nevada.

Careful plans were made. Many workers would be needed. They would have to be willing to work in terrible heat. Sometimes the temperatures in the canyon went up to 120°F. Workers would have to climb the tall canyon walls and move tons of materials. They would have to build small dams to move the river out of the way so they could drill **tunnels** in the canyon walls.

How would all of this get done? In 1931, more than 1,000 men were hired for the job. More workers would come later. They would work seven days a week, day and night, for five long years to finish Hoover Dam.

DID YOU KNOW?
Workers were paid 50 cents an hour, which was a lot of money at the time.

Man-made tunnel in Black Canyon

7

The Plan Takes Shape

For more than two years, workers drilled and tunneled through the rock walls. They cleared away loose stones and dirt and pumped the river water away.

Other workers worked far above the ground. Their job was to prepare the canyon walls. Sometimes they liked to show off for the many visitors who came to watch the dam being built.

Canyon wall worker during Hoover Dam construction

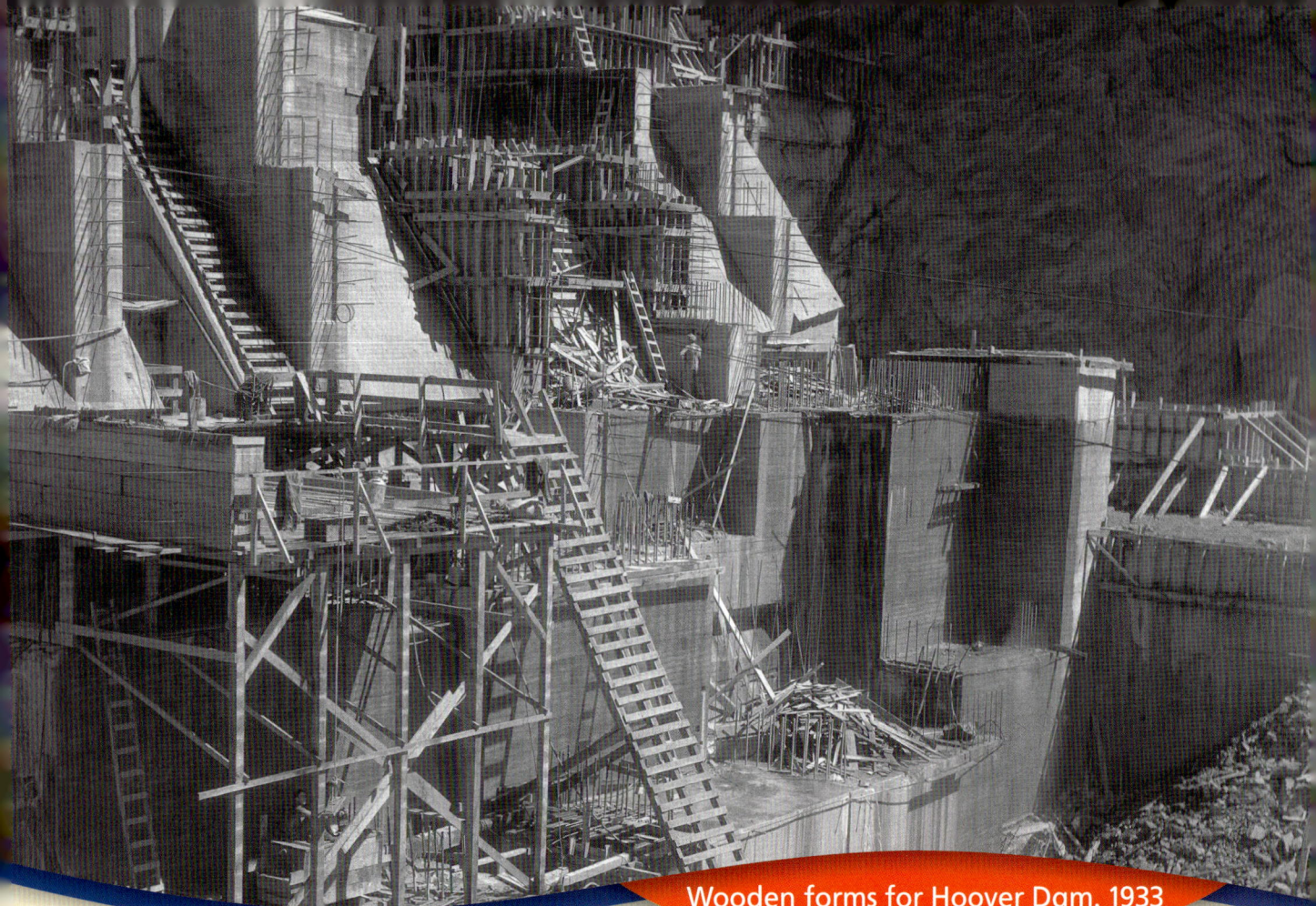

At last, the ground and the canyon walls were ready. Next, they needed enormous amounts of concrete to build the dam. The concrete would have to be poured a little at a time.

Steel cables carried huge buckets of wet concrete. The concrete was poured into wooden **forms**. The forms held the concrete until it dried into giant blocks. Each form was as big as a house. Day after day, more blocks were added.

But Hoover Dam needed more than concrete blocks. This huge dam needed to pump water from the Colorado River to faraway farms and homes. It also needed special runoff pipes to keep floods from happening again.

A **power plant** was going to be built, too. Energy from the rushing river would be used to make electricity. Wires had to be hung for miles and miles to carry the electrical power to towns and cities.

There was even going to be a road that went over the top of the dam so that it could be used as a bridge. There was so much work to do!

DID YOU KNOW?

Fifteen swimming pools worth of water can flow through Hoover Dam's power plant in just one second.

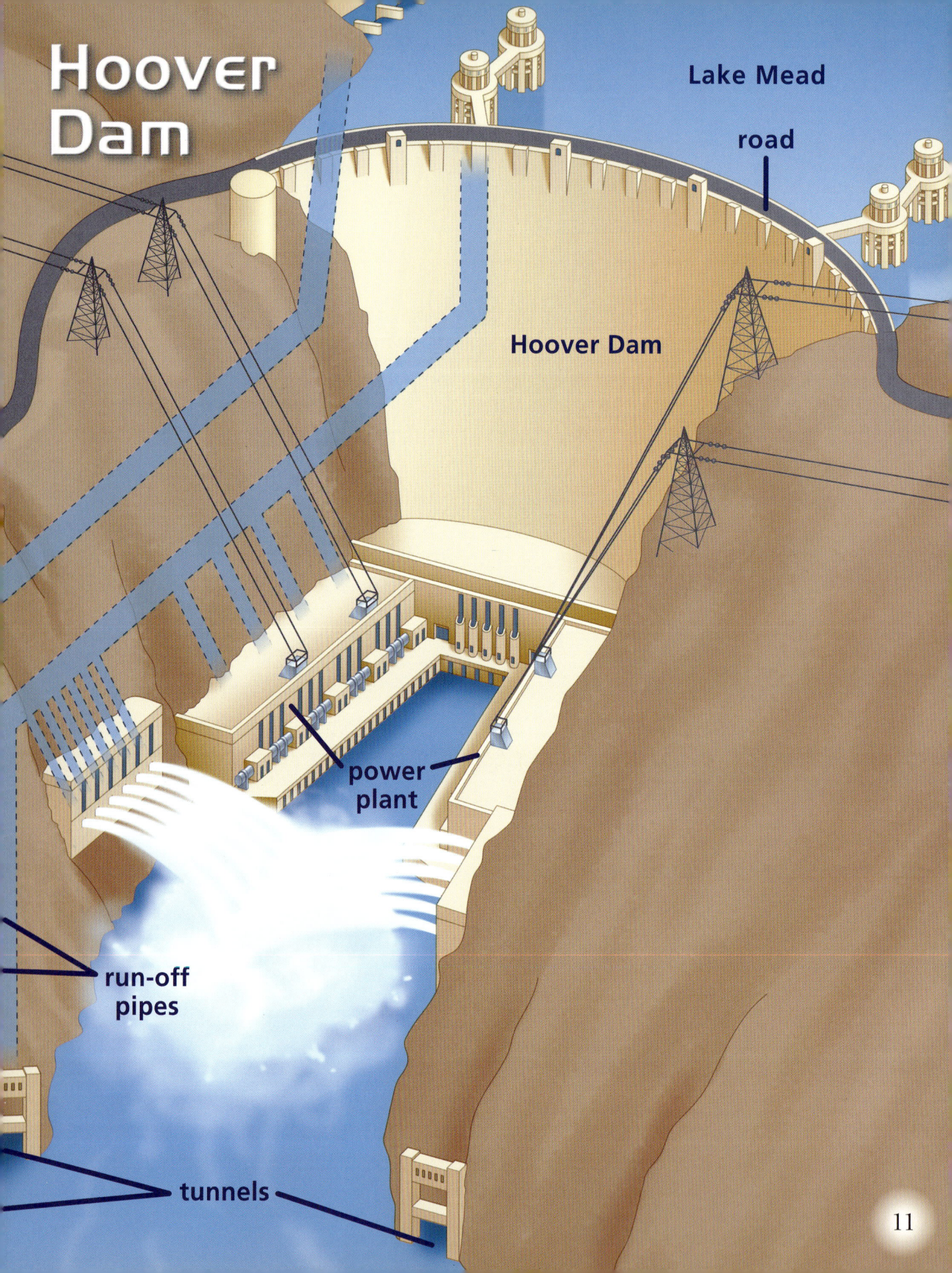

Hoover Dam

Lake Mead

road

Hoover Dam

power plant

run-off pipes

tunnels

11

Success!

By September 30, 1935, almost all of the work had been finished. On that day, 20,000 people gathered around Black Canyon to hear President Franklin D. Roosevelt honor the workers who built Hoover Dam. The dam was named after Herbert Hoover, who was president when the project started.

Hoover Dam, 1935

After the dam was in place, Lake Mead filled up behind it. Water was pumped out to the southwestern United States and even into parts of Mexico. The dam's power plant began making electricity.

People were amazed at the courage and hard work it had taken to build this enormous dam. Today, Hoover Dam is still one of the most impressive structures in the United States!

Heights of Famous Structures

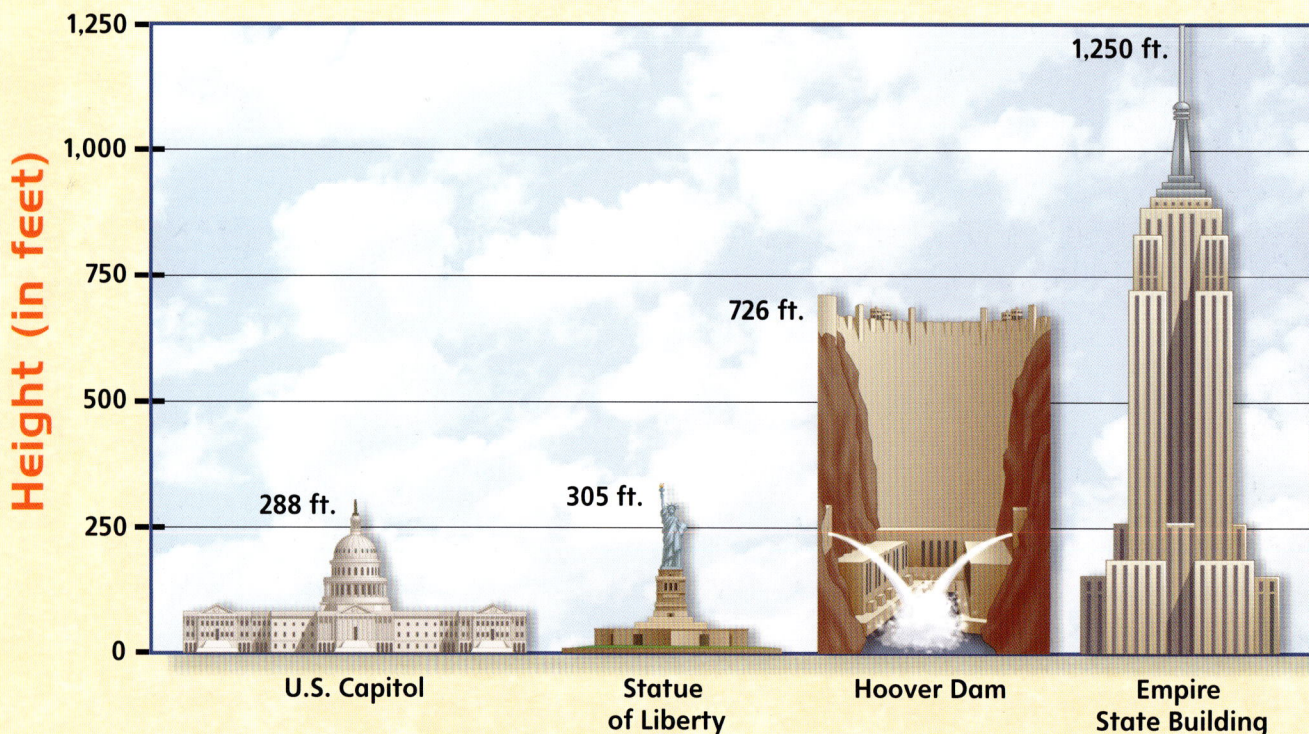

Bar graph showing Height (in feet) for famous structures:
- U.S. Capitol: 288 ft.
- Statue of Liberty: 305 ft.
- Hoover Dam: 726 ft.
- Empire State Building: 1,250 ft.

Famous Structures

Because of Hoover Dam, we have many more farms in the southwestern United States. Cities like Los Angeles, California get clean drinking water and electrical power. People no longer worry as much about floods from the Colorado River sweeping away their homes and businesses.

Los Angeles, California

Just as people thought, the dam brought new roads and towns, and the desert was filled with people.

Who knew 6.6 million tons of concrete could change the lives of so many people!

Glossary

canyon   a deep, long hole in the earth made by the flow of rushing water

concrete   a mix of cement, sand, rock, and water that hardens into a strong stone

dam   something built to block the flow of water

ditches   long, narrow holes dug into the earth to direct the flow of water

flood   extra water that rushes out of a river or other body of water and covers land

forms   large wooden frames used to hold concrete in a certain shape while it dries

government   a group of people who have the power to make laws for an area

power plant   a place where electricity is made from another source of energy, like flowing water.

tunnel   a long passage, usually underground

Index

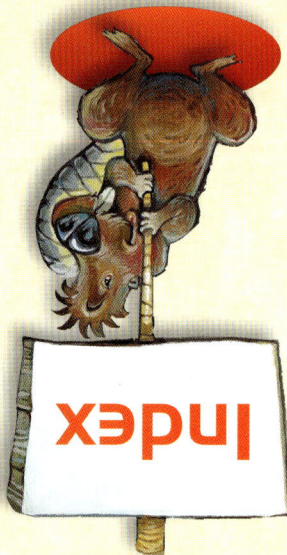